Re-Orthodox

Rediscover the Truth and Wonder of
the Christian Faith

D1738540

Jacob Schmelzer

ReOrthodox

Copyright © 2011 Zoe Bible College
All rights reserved.
Requests for information should be sent to:
Zoe Bible College Publications
2715 Table Rock Rd. Medford, OR 97501

ISBN: 0-9846602-0-8
ISBN-13: 978-0-9846602-0-9

Cover Design: Natalie Schmelzer
Photography: Bethany Schmelzer

This book is dedicated to the love of my life, Bethany, and to the love of our lives, Evelyn Joy.

Table of Contents

Re-Orthodox

1

A Fantastic Reality

It has often been said that what you don't know can't hurt you. As you and I both know that statement is completely and categorically false. It is well known that what you don't know can, and often does, hurt you. I have never met a person who, knowing they would be crushed by a piano falling from the sky if they went outside that day, would still take a walk in the park. Fate can work its business only because we are uninformed of its purpose. Fate has never made an appointment with me for good or evil. I would always show up for the good ones and neglect the bad. Ignorance of what will happen today, tomorrow, or even the next day is a fact we must face. It will almost always be what you don't know, that which you did not prepare for, that hurts you.

In light of that rather unpleasant thought I have written this book. If an unpleasant fate is looming in your future do you not wish to know of it? Would you not wish someone to forewarn you that something unpleasant was coming if they knew beforehand? I believe that I have that information, but it isn't what you may think. I don't have any prediction of a coming apocalypse, of worldwide terror and trouble. I don't have a prognostication of coming calamity for you or your family. I simply want you to reconsider something you may have written off a long time ago as an unsuitable answer to life's questions, the Christian faith. Perhaps what you believe about God, yourself, and the world around you has been subverted by an enemy that hates you, despises your soul, and wishes to destroy you.

This might all sound a bit theatrical, and it is. The fact, though, is that our lives are a drama, being played out on a cosmic stage. There are parts being played; of heroes and villains alike. There are great sweeping tragedies and almost unbelievable comedies of love and laughter taking place every day all around the world. Is it so unbelievable to think that maybe it all has a purpose? That maybe all of what we see happening around us is some great story being played out.

A Fantastic Reality

Now, we know that we are not characters in a story, at least not like in a child's bedtime story. You and I are not fictional characters. No, we are very real. We feel deeply, love passionately, and grieve desperately. We struggle for meaning, for contentment, and for joy. We fight wars for freedom and trade empires for ideas. We exhibit almost reckless faith in the face of brutal facts. We are not fictional characters. We are alive. But we are characters nonetheless, living in a real story, or rather, a true story.

This is a self-evident truth. When we tell a child they are wrong to fear a monster under their bed we are correcting their assumption of the monsters location, not its existence. There are such things as monsters. Just because squids, scorpions, and spiders have all been studied in a laboratory doesn't take away the fact they are still monsters. We commit a silly fallacy when we treat the world as if it were anything other than a true story. We act as if the real world is less strange or unbelievable than a story merely because it is real. But think back to the first time you ever saw something in real life that you never knew existed before.

The first time I watched a program about the kinds of creatures that inhabit the deep sea beyond the reach of sunlight I was horrified at the monsters that I discovered to be living down there! The real sea monsters are no less scary then the Kraken or Moby Dick. Our wildest fantasies are not anymore wild than our realities. We simply see reality with jaded eyes. We take our world, our story, for granted.

We act as if fighting a lion in this world is somehow less frightening then St. George fighting a dragon in another. One is real, one is fictitious, but the courage in both stories is equally real. In fact, courage is what is most real, for it transcends both worlds.

It is an interesting phenomenon that we need to face a dragon in our fantasies so that we can face a lion in reality. To really see our own story we must first see someone else's. It is often assumed that fantasies blind us from reality, but might it not be the other way round? I'm not saying that reality is an illusion, or that we are the fantasy and fantasy the reality. No, we have already determined that we are alive. We exist. We inhabit a tangible physical space somewhere in the cosmos. What I mean is that we are often blind to the truth because we are contented with facts.

This is one of the truly great tragedies of modernity. Man has stopped hungering for truth because he has grown fat on facts. The modern age has been one gluttonous feast of knowledge that has only led to dissatisfaction. Postmodernism is no better. It is merely the regurgitation of modernism. The action was not good. The reaction is no better. It has often been this way in history. Man has swallowed fallacies, spit them out, and gobbled them up again, only to repeat the process. This is what we call progress. But it is really nothing more than foolish and arrogant grasping.

Why is this so? It is because we crave answers. The shape of our heart is a question mark. We want to know why. Why do we exist? Why is my life like this? Why?

'*Why*' is probably not as important of a question as either '*What*' or '*Who*,' but it is always the first one we ask. There is something in our hearts that longs for meaning. We want to know why. This is probably one of the reasons why many people pass by, or pass through, the Christian faith without sticking around. Christianity doesn't start by telling us '*Why*.' It starts by telling us '*Who*.' Then it tells us '*What*.' And then finally, in the end, it tells us '*Why*.' This can be frustrating. I know, I am a Christian and it frustrates me. I want to know '*Why*' as much as you do. God, why? Universe, why? Fate, why? This is simply our condition. I think this is what prompted Augustine to say, "Thou hast made us for thyself, O Lord, and our hearts are restless until they find their rest in thee."

The Christian answer to man's questions is that our unfulfilled condition can only be fulfilled by God. But this answer makes people uncomfortable because we don't want a '*Who*.' We want a '*Why*.' Make no mistake; there is a big difference between them. A '*Who*' means a person, like we are. And we aren't stupid, we know what that means.

A Fantastic Reality

Persons are emotional, complicated, and demanding. Persons feel deeply, love passionately, and grieve desperately, remember? Persons confront us in the plane of reality and cannot be ignored or explained away. To do so would be to explain ourselves away. To deny a Person would be to deny ourselves. But we don't want a Person. We want a '*Why*.' A '*Why*' is abstract, impersonal, and flexible. A '*Why*' can be shaped and molded into a pleasing answer. We have desperately hoped that we won't have to change and that the answer to '*Why*' will just make it all better.

All of mankind's efforts to find an answer have been directed at finding the '*Why*,' the silver bullet that will kill the beast. The struggle in our heart screams for resolution but we cannot solve the enigma. The beast is within. The question, the discontent, is inescapable. It's why Paul said, "O wretched man that I am! Who will deliver me from this body of death?" We feel our discontent eating us alive on the inside. But it manifests on the outside.

We are sick, but it's our marriages, friendships, and careers that suffer. We cannot fix ourselves and even this reality irks us. It has been said that he who has himself for a physician has a fool for a physician. But we want to fix ourselves. We want an answer from the inside, from ourselves, to fix our outside, but the answer we really need comes from the outside and works on the inside.

This is the beginning of the Christian answer to man's dilemma. Man demands an answer. He shouts at the sky and is given a seed. He looks at it, turns it over in his hand, and is often unimpressed. Christianity looks unappealing, weak, and even foolish to people who have grown accustomed to humanistic sophistry but there is power in it. Like the power of a seed, it starts small, even weakly, but grows into something mighty.

But Christianity's answer for us is not abstract and impersonal. When we ask for an answer we are introduced to a person, but not just any person, to God Himself. Does it seem strange to talk of God, wanting to know you, wanting to communicate with you? Does it seem like a fantasy? Perhaps it is because our story is so fantastic that we must invent fantasies to gain perspective. Could not Zeus, Athena, and Apollo simply be characters in a story that someone told, and maybe even came to believe in, as a way to gain perspective on their own story?

Christianity's great foe isn't paganism, for paganism at least recognizes *some* God. We look back into history with disdain at the pagans, not realizing that they may have been closer to the truth than we are. They recognized the story, the great undercurrent of history, the power of the unknown working behind the scenes. They recognized that there was a power higher than themselves, even if they failed to recognize the Most High.

In the modern age we have run as far from the beliefs of the ancients as possible, but we have only started new cults. The religious servants of knowledge and experience are as misguided as the servants of Zeus, perhaps more. In this modern age we have shut our eyes in the hope that we would not be seen. We don't want the answer to be a '*Who.*' We don't want a person. We don't want God. We have buttressed ourselves against the tide of truth by piling up defenses like sandbags erected to stop a flood. But ultimately the walls must come down. Though we may choose not to see, we are not hidden from the eternal gaze. We are not hidden from the eyes of fire. You can close your eyes, but closing your eyes does not make you invisible.

2

The Old Road

Alas, I am sure you know of what I speak. I speak of God. I speak of religion and tradition. I speak of Orthodoxy, a dead word for many, but still poignant. I speak of return and re-acquaintance with a road that you may have once traveled upon, but have now left behind for paths that seemed more promising. You may have abandoned the old road, deeming it familiar, tired, and old; but what if the old road is only old because it leads to ancient and eternal secrets? Who's to say that the old road isn't old for the very reason that it was the first and greatest road? How many unsuspecting citizens of Rome tread daily upon the paths of great emperors and mighty legions from the ancient and glorious past without recognition or regard? How could it be known that the same tired lane that carried us to school, to church, and to our homes also led to adventure and peril?

And, where would such a road take us? At first it would seem to take us backwards, through the places we'd already passed. It would take us through both pleasant and unpleasant places. Eventually we'd come to where we started, maybe a happy home, maybe hell. But around the bend from that place where it all began for us we'd see a path that stretched all the way back to the dawn of time itself. We've heard of this road, haven't we? This is the road of history; tread by those that have come before, stretching for eons into the distant past. What might we find if we traveled down this path?

"Certainly," you might say, "there is nothing down that road that hasn't been tried before. We have progressed so much. Why return down that path seeking answers that must certainly lie in the future?" This sentiment is often heard. The myth of progress says that the future must hold the secrets we seek. How is this known? Does not history establish a trajectory for the future? It would seem that the writer of Ecclesiastes was on to something when he said that there was nothing new under the sun. And we, even in this advanced place in history, are still under the same sun. Its tireless beams beat upon us, just as they did upon the ancient ones who also looked to the future for answers.

Yet here we are, peering back through history at them, still asking the same questions. And might we also look into the future for answers and find the same result as our forebears? What if our technology advanced to the place where we could peel back the curtain of our future? We would only see people, perhaps with better technology, but people nonetheless, with questions still burning in their hearts.

But if the future holds no promise and the past has been tried, where do we turn? Man's enigma remains. Our mortality rests heavily on our shoulders and we strain under the weight of our struggle. We are a strange case. It seems that we are forever doomed to wander up and down this road, never knowing, never understanding where we should go. Do we press towards the future or look to the past? Do we need more technology, more knowledge, or more time? Are we a race of beings full of unfulfilled promise, destined for some undiscovered purpose, yet doomed to never find an answer?

No, we must return, for surely we have missed something on the journey. We must go back down the old road, and we mustn't stop until we find what we are looking for. We must travel to the beginning of it all. Surely that is where we will find answers.

One of the great follies of the modern world is that we only go back so far into history in our search for answers. We query Camus, Nietzsche, and Voltaire. We seek answers from Aristotle and Alexander. We study Caesar and Churchill but we still don't find the answers we seek. We have drunk those wells dry and yet our thirst is not quenched.

We must go back even further, to where the old road is rough and barely passable. Back, back before history. Back, even before time itself. It is in this place, formless and void, that all men must forge a belief. For it is here that the old road ends, or I should say, where it really begins. Like ancient mapmakers considering the edge of a flat world, we cannot fathom what lies beyond this point.

The Old Road

It is at this great precipice where we must leave aside our calculators and computers. These tools will do us no good here. Only courage, conviction, and faith will help us here, for it is here where all of us must take a flying leap into the abyss and hope our feet meet something solid. Science has no answer here. Religion has no answer here. They do not exist here. They have not been created. We are at the very beginning.

It is here at the start of the old road where everything that we know began. This is the source. It is here we must choose what we believe about the world and ourselves. It is here we must make a choice. Is it something or someone? This question is really where it starts for us. What kind of a world do we really live in? We know that we are here, that our history has happened. After all, we traveled down the old road to get here.

What we know for sure is that we actually do exist. The very act of doubting that fundamental reality discredits the doubt itself. What we must determine is what caused everything to happen, if there was any cause at all. We must determine what existed at the beginning.

Two options present themselves to us at this juncture. We are living in a universe made of matter and energy which may or may not have a supernatural element as well. So, to account for this universe we must either decide if it is personal or impersonal. This means that we must either choose the eternal self-existence of matter and energy. That is, that matter and energy have always been. Or, we must accept that the universe is not eternal and that it was caused. Its existence is not in question. It either came to be or it always was.

But there is more. Beyond the purely material nature of the universe are the deep abiding questions of the human heart. Why am *I* here? Why do I suffer pain and experience joy? Does my existence have a purpose and if so, what is it?

As we ponder questions like these we are only joining the great host of humanity in asking the fundamental questions of life. We spoke of these questions previously. These are the questions that cause our hearts to ache with expectation of an answer. We want to know '*Why.*' As I said earlier, the Christian story doesn't start with an answer for the '*Why.*' It starts with a '*Who.*' Before answering the existential questions of the heart, the Christian story deals with the nature of the universe itself and how it came to be. It sets the stage for the great drama of humanity before introducing it and resolving it.

The Christian story starts with the shockingly simple pronouncement of God's existence. It then goes on to describe who this God is. He is omnipotent, omniscient, and omnipresent. He is infinite and transcendent, but He is also personal and immanent. And, I think most importantly for us, He is good.

Please take the time to rid your mind of the image of an old man with a scowl on his face and a lightning bolt in his hand. This image is not wholly corrupt. In fact, the problem is not that it conveys too much. Instead, it conveys far too little. When we picture God as only a God of judgment we have not made Him too terrible. We have rather made Him less terrible than He really is. For God does not need anger and lightning to inspire awe. He is pure love and burning light which no man can hide from. God is something more terrifying than lightning. He is perfect goodness. Our darkened souls cower before His awesome perfection and we will one day have to stand before Him.

But God also loves, perfectly and passionately. He is always reaching for us. This God is both beautiful and bold, awe inspiring, and yet approachable. God is a father whose hand brings both correction and protection.

It is this God that Christianity presents at the start. It is this God who rushes into history as the Creator of everything. It is this God who appears uncaused and unexplained "In the beginning," and then starts to tell the story. It is this God who we find at the start of the old road.

3

A Fork and a Fall

If it seems somewhat scandalous to simply believe in God at the beginning of the old road that's because it is. It is sudden. It is shocking to our modern nerves. It rings of blind faith and belief without evidence. But isn't that where we all stand? At the precipice of origins all men must forge a belief. The Christian believes in an eternal God, the atheist believes in eternal matter and energy. Neither of these beliefs can be empirically verified but don't be alarmed. Both have reasons. We can follow the road forward to find these reasons.

The only catch is that the road forks here. Yes, right at the beginning, the road takes two diverging paths. If God exists, then we must take that path. If God does not exist then we must take another. Each path leads us to a far different destination. And remember, we are not talking about fictional roads. We are talking about life, about history, and about reality itself. We must choose our road carefully for it is that road which we ourselves must journey on.

It is the joy of certain mean spirited pseudo-intellectuals to act as if all roads of belief are mere fiction, that the realities people encounter are fantasies. This is not so and we all know it. When a person chooses a path of belief the perils they face are real. The implications of beliefs and worldviews are not fictional. They are fact. It is for this reason that we should not choose a road of belief flippantly or casually.

Each of us must choose a path and then follow it to its end. I ask you now to walk with me down the path of Christianity for a time. You can turn back if you wish but I want to show you what's around the bend.

As we begin to walk along the path of Christianity we are met with a glorious beginning and then a sudden and arresting fall. The first pages of the Bible reflect this abrupt transition. According to the Christian story human history is not a gradually ascending, ever progressing movement. The universe was not brought along like an infant slowly growing, slowly developing to maturity.

No. The beginning was gloriously sudden and suddenly glorious. God embarked upon six days of explosive imagination culminating in man's creation. And it was not a baby, helpless and dependant, that was first established in Eden. It was Adam, first father of our race, full grown and fully endowed with the capacity to steward God's creation. Adam was placed like a king in a beautiful garden with his queen Eve, drawn from his side to stand by his side.

They stood together, in innocence without credulity and authority without tyranny. They walked among the splendors of Eden, enjoying without spoiling. And they talked, in the cool of the day with their Maker.

The glory of Eden almost seems too fantastic to be real, but it was. It was as the glory of the morning sun which rises to its throne in the sky without pride or pretense. The sun rises regally to take its rightful place and is utterly without competition. Nothing could ever compete, not the moon, not Jupiter, Venus, or Mars. As the sun is the glory of the sky so was Eden the glory of man. It was our height of heights.

For this reason, its fall was all the greater. The mighty falls of empires throughout history paled in comparison. The falls of Egypt, Babylon, Greece, and Rome were mere stumbles compared to the violence of Eden's. The empires of man's design were built from the refuse of mighty Eden. Their towers of strength were built upon Eden's ashes. Babel, which reached for heaven, did not even reach Eden. The sun never set upon the British Empire but the empire of Eden hosted the Maker of the sun in its garden.

All the serenity and nobility of Eden was shattered in a momentous catastrophe. Perhaps the memory of Atlantis' fall is a shadow cast by Eden's. What, in one moment was everything, was in the next, nothing. But Atlantis only fell into the sea. Eden fell into oblivion. One is in some way recoverable while the other is not. Atlantis fell from our embrace but we fell from Eden's. The bitterness of the loss of Eden was the sting of eternal exile brought on by rebellion.

A Fork and a Fall

The great tragedy that took place in Eden haunts our imagination even now. It was the scene of a horrendous battle between heaven and hell. Sadly Adam, the emperor of noble Eden, chose to rally to hell's banner instead of heaven's. Adam, the father of our race and the bearer of our destiny, allowed an enemy to penetrate his realm. He allowed this enemy to speak treason against heaven amongst the hallowed boughs of Eden. His queen was deceived but Adam chose willingly to enter into alliance with the prince of death. With one bite he declared war against heaven and brought Eden crashing down around them.

As what had been forbidden was embraced the war that began in heaven crashed to earth like a meteor, destroying Eden in its fury. The wicked adversary was unmasked and cursed; the sovereigns of Eden cast out and brought low. But even in that moment, when earth lost its innocence and the laughter of hell was heard echoing among the trees of Eden, all was not lost. Though the father and mother of our race were abased, they were not abandoned. While hell's fire and heaven's fury collided around them they were shielded by the one they had betrayed. The world had changed in an instant but God did not leave them alone.

Their road would now be difficult, full of danger and disaster, as ours is, but God would guide them with a promise. Though the opulence of Eden was no more He promised that Eden would rise again on the shoulders of a new King. This promise, like the last remaining ember of a once roaring fire, became the hope of a new day. Though the once bright world had become hopelessly dim a spark could be seen, small but clear. And it wouldn't die…

But the heart of man, once exposed to the fire of hell, would not be satisfied with heaven's embers. The lust of the flesh, lust of the eyes, and the pride of life pulled upon our forebears and they took up arms against heaven once again. The war begun in heaven, and now fought upon the earth, would bring blight upon the world. And yet, the ember of Eden's hope still glowed in the hearts of some.

God, seated upon His heavenly throne, did not retreat from the battle or pull back His hand of blessing from those that were faithful to Him.

A Fork and a Fall

Though it seemed His greatest treasure had become His greatest loss He waited to unveil His greatest sacrifice and His greatest victory. As time passed and the road grew longer and longer God waited, and waited still. Though the world seemed to come more and more under the sway of hell God waited. But then, when the moment was right, God planted a seed.

Whereas the first Adam was planted like a mighty oak in the garden, full grown and mature, the second Adam was revealed in weakness. The story of Eden's grandeur is a tragedy. It is the story of man's glory full grown and his failure and fall from that grace. But the coming of the second Adam took the opposite course. If Eden was God's original dream for man it had been turned upside down. The world had become what it was never intended to be.

All that was wrong with the world became commonplace. Injustice and insanity took control. Man had been given the highest place of authority. His fall thus opened wide the door for evil to enter. The heart of man, once the seat of grace, became the source of disgrace. The world was upside down from the fall, maybe because it was still falling.

The story of the first Adam was of the highest height of man becoming the lowest low. The story of the second Adam is of the lowest becoming the highest and the weakest becoming the strongest. If the world had been turned upside down it was now being turned right side up again. Eden was full of strength and glory. Its splendor shone in the dawning light of the universe. Adam was born in the light of morning but Jesus was born in the dark of night. Adam was given the strength and power of the firstborn man. Jesus was given the body of an infant. Adam's first breath was the air of Eden. Jesus' was the air of a stable in lowly Bethlehem.

Without pomp, privilege, or provenance the King of Glory arrived on mortal soil clothed in mortal flesh. Quiet as His coming was, all of hell was set at alarm. The last ember of Eden flashed brilliantly in a Judean sky, a star, shining on a boy in a manger. An emissary, not of Eden, but of heaven itself, had come to avenge the fall, come to set the captives free.

4

A Pause on the Path

We must pause upon the path for a moment because I can feel the questions burning away in your head. "Is he getting ahead of himself here?" "Is there even a God?" The story that I have just begun to tell you—the Christian story (what I believe to be the true story of reality)—is only as reliable as the foundation it is built upon. If the Christian God doesn't exist then it is all just a lot of fluff. For this reason it is pertinent that we stop and examine the essential question here and now. Before proceeding any further let us examine the question of God.

This may seem strange to you but I beg just another moment of your time. If our reaction to the question of God's existence is a kind of horror at dipping into something mystical or spiritual I must assert that this is only a rather recent exception that has crept into our thinking.

I hope to show you that it is our reaction to the question of God's existence in modern times that is odd, even alien, to what people have believed throughout history. If we look back in time we will see people who accepted that there were powers at work in the universe both higher and greater than themselves. The civilizations in existence at the beginning of history accepted the gods.

Their belief in the gods exhibited their acceptance of divinity and there can be no Divine without divinity. The ancients recognized a power at work in the universe that was beyond the universe itself. The human-like gods of the pagans were simply the first attempt at denying the authority of the eternal God. People often seek to make God in their own image instead of accepting that they are made in His.

This was man's rebellion, part of the war against heaven. Throughout history, the great pagans sought to soften the divine claim of rule by humanizing the gods. A god that is just like us is not worthy of our worship. A human-like god is only a god because of their power. They rule by force and can only be viewed as a tyrant, feared but not loved. But even this poisoned view of God had its merit. A Creator, a personal force at work behind the scenes, answers so many questions.

What of the modern age? Modernity has not only taught us to love facts above truth; it has also shaped our thinking mechanism. Ask a dozen people on the street how they determine what is true and a majority will spit out something vaguely resembling the scientific process. By the scientific process I am referring to the scientific method of testing a hypothesis, as in a laboratory, through empirical observation. Empirical observation has become engrained in the modern brain as a fool proof method of knowledge. But there are many questions that cannot be answered in this way.

Theology and philosophy walk in fields that empiricism cannot. Science can answer the '*What's*' but not the '*Why's.*' For the '*Why's*' we must turn elsewhere. Allow me to briefly demonstrate this idea. If we were to come upon a room where a man had been found dead we could use our empirical sense to see the brutal facts. Let's play detective shall we?

In our imaginary scene we are presented with an empty room where we find a bloody candlestick lying next to a dead man with a gruesome head wound. Our empirical observation tells us only the facts. There is a dead man and a bloody candlestick. To draw any other conclusions we would need to leave observation behind. We would have to move on to reasoning. We would ask: "Why are there a dead man and a bloody candlestick here together? Is this the scene of a murder or an accidental death?" Our minds would begin to grind away at the problem set before us.

If we were good detectives we would search for other evidence that could help shed light on the unfortunate situation. But alas, there is nothing else in the room, just a dead man and a candlestick. From what can be observed we know the '*What*' (a dead man and a candlestick) but not the '*Why*' (why is there a dead man here?).

A Pause on the Path

Our empirical observation has come to its limits—at least in this case. Empirical observation and inductive/deductive reasoning are at the mercy of the available evidence. This case could easily be solved if the proper evidence were available. Let us say that a note detailing an angry wife's crime of passion against her husband came to light. Then we would have both the '*Why*' and '*What*'. But in our simulated crime scene that evidence is not available.

We have just the facts, the brutal disturbing facts. But what should we do? There is another quandary that immediately presents itself. We cannot be satisfied with only the facts. We need the truth. "Why is this man dead? Was he murdered? Who is he?" The questions abound. The facts are known but it is the truth that is the real object of our desire. We must know '*Why*,' and naked empiricism has not given us the answer. It cannot.

Now let us apply this example to the question of God. Like detectives we have arrived at the scene of the crime, the universe, and are confronted by the facts. Though the scene is infinitesimally more complex than our imaginary one of the previous paragraph the same principles apply.

Empirical observation can give us facts about the universe but it cannot give us the truth. And it is the truth that we require. Why is the universe here? Where did it come from? Why do I exist? Questions like these are metaphysical in nature and they demand a metaphysical answer. As we have seen, the raw facts cannot give us the truth. We could discover all of the '*What's*' in the universe and still not have the '*Why's.*' But that doesn't excuse us from our search. Our restless hearts and inquisitive minds will not be satisfied with just the facts.

As we observe the universe, and our existence within it, we are met with a reality that must be accounted for, reality itself. And reality is much more than matter. In fact, a great deal of meaningful human existence is predicated upon immaterial things such as thought, emotion, and imagination.

All people must give an account for reality. One may choose to believe in God's existence or not but everyone must choose. This choice is the beginning of what is known as a worldview. A worldview is a system of presuppositions about reality, truth, and morality that each individual holds either consciously or subconsciously. Our worldview is the lens through which we view all of life and we all have one.

In the Christian worldview God's existence is presupposed. It is by the light of His existence that Christians interpret life. God is the first fact of Christianity. In an atheistic worldview there is no God and yet the universe, and humanity, both still exist. Both worldviews are tasked with answering the same questions about the origin of the universe and the meaning of life.

The atheist and the Christian are both faced with the existential and philosophical quandaries of life. We must all deal with the enigmas of meaning, suffering, love, and death. The full breadth and depth of what it means to be human confronts us every day. Theories meet their match in reality. Every ideology and philosophy must be lived out. There is no escaping this.

So what story are we to tell, or be told about life then? Both material and immaterial concerns must be accounted for in this story. It has to account for all of reality—the '*Why's*' as well as the '*What's*.' We can't hide behind inadequate answers any longer. If science cannot tell us '*Why*' then we must stop asking it to.

To be clear, the problem has nothing to do with science. Science is a useful tool for observing the universe. Furthermore, there is nothing antithetical about faith and science. My intention is not to create a dichotomy between them. I believe it would be a false dichotomy. There has always been a place for science within the Christian worldview. In fact, the scientific pursuit only makes sense from the perspective of the Christian worldview. Christianity tells the story of a universe that functions according to a pattern of designed laws, the laws of science. If the atheist is allowed to deny the Lawgiver then he should give up his belief in laws. For the atheist the laws of science should really become the 'random, yet inexplicably consistent occurrences of science.'

A Pause on the Path

The atheist, according to his worldview, doesn't have a good reason for believing that the universe functions and will continue to function according to set laws and patterns. Why should it? Why would a universe with a random beginning suddenly begin to exhibit properties of order? If the universe was birthed in chance, how and why do we observe a system of uniform natural causes?

Why would an atheist ever have the faith to walk out of their house expecting that gravity would continue to keep them anchored to the earth? Perhaps a little of the same random chance that was necessary for the emergence of the universe according to their worldview would kick in and gravity would suddenly reverse itself sending them flying into space.

I am not saying that this is likely to happen. In fact, it won't happen. This can be affirmed with confidence according to the Christian worldview. It is preposterous to think that random reversals of the natural order would occur for no reason in a system designed to function according to set laws. It is for this very reason that atheism's proposal about the universe is inadequate. When you purposely introduce the necessity of chance and randomness into your explanation of the universe you cannot simply wave it off later when it becomes inconvenient.

The question of God's existence is a simple question with a rather complex answer. The idea that God exists might be rather hard to accept but what of the alternative? Faith is in some ways a choice but so is doubt. To believe in God or deny Him is to make a commitment towards a particular worldview.

The questions are the same for both sides. Our universe must be explained in some way or another. The denial of God's existence is not an adequate solution in and of itself. It introduces new questions without necessarily answering the old ones. With this understanding in mind we can begin to approach the questions the universe lays before us with at least some level of objectivity. All worldviews must give an account of reality. Also, all worldviews must establish a framework of knowledge through which our questions can be phrased, understood, and eventually answered—a way to determine what is true. And lastly, all worldviews must touch on the existential realities such as good and evil, joy and suffering, and the meaning of life. These questions cannot be left unanswered by any worldview that would seek to give humanity an accurate and complete view of life.

Our reality confronts us constantly with the question of its own existence. It is a question that cannot be ignored. Though the wise answer the question with great trepidation it is only left unanswered at great peril; for life surges ahead at the speed of time and we are carried along in its current. Our day of reckoning is always drawing nearer.

5

Following the Fork

In chapter three I spoke of a fork in the road that we come to as we walk down the old road. We walked a little way down the path of Christian history but it's time to walk down the other fork to see what we can discover. According to the Christian story the universe had a beginning, due to the creative action of God. If we walk down the other fork we find quite a different perspective. In the last chapter we examined the question, "Is there a God?" The fork in the road that you will take is dependent upon your answer to that question. In this chapter we will assume that your answer is no.

By answering in the negative to the question of God's existence we take up a position. This is an important thing to understand before we proceed. Disbelief and doubt are choices just as sure as faith and belief are. Disbelief is not a neutral position. Neither is doubt. In fact, neutrality, when it comes to life and its fundamental questions, does not exist.

Every choice, whether towards God or away from Him, is a step in a certain direction. With that in mind, let us proceed.

By following the fork of disbelief in a creator God at the beginning of the old road we come to some difficult ground right away. If nothing or no one *created* the universe that we know to exist then how did it come to exist at all? We are given two explanations, or choices, with regards to this conundrum. Either the universe has always been, or, the universe had a beginning. If we choose the first option; that is—that the universe has always been— then that reality must become the foundation of our worldview. The eternal universe becomes the backdrop for our existence and our existence must be interpreted in light of it.

Option two—the idea that the universe had a beginning at some point but without a personal cause—also must become the foundation of our worldview if we choose it. Let us see where each might lead us. First, an eternal universe doesn't seem to square very well with the universe that we inhabit.

Take the existence of *Time* for instance. The concept of time is rooted in the idea of a beginning and an end. You cannot measure time without some standard to measure it against. In our universe we measure the passing of time against the backdrop of a solar system, galaxy, and universe that is in motion. Let me give you another example.

Imagine that you are sailing upon an infinite ocean. The ocean has no boundaries, no shorelines. How would you measure your progress across this ocean? You have no point of departure or destination from which to determine your progress. You can sail for weeks but you are not getting closer to your destination or further from your starting point. They don't exist. There is no way to quantify infinity. This is what is known as the impossibility of an infinite regress. It is one reason why the belief in an eternal universe (consisting of matter and energy) doesn't make much sense.

The idea of an eternal universe contradicts the laws of science; e.g. the laws of thermodynamics. Our personal experience in the universe also contradicts the idea of an eternal universe. The fact that we are alive at a certain point in time demonstrates that there is such a thing as time itself. How could you live another year and measure it's passing in an infinite universe? It would not be possible. How do you add one more of something to an infinite number?

So what of the other possibility? Perhaps the universe had an *impersonal* (purely natural, consisting solely of matter and energy) cause. This idea actually makes more sense because everything that can be observed in the universe has or had a cause at some point. It has not been my particular experience to observe objects or beings randomly appear out of thin air in front of me. When I see people walking around town I assume that there is an explanation for their existence. They must have had parents, and their parents must have had parents, and their parents must have had…and, well, you get the idea. It's the same thing with plants and animals. They have an explanation, a reason for existing.

What about inanimate objects like rocks? Do rocks simple appear out of thin air? No, they are explainable as well. It appears that everything in our universe has an explanation rooted in its cause. Everything that exists is dependent upon something else for an explanation of its existence. What we eventually end up with is the proverbial chicken or egg debate when it comes to the universe's existence. What came first? As stated earlier, the idea that the universe had a first cause, whether personal or impersonal, makes more sense than the belief in an eternal or infinite universe. But what makes more sense: a personal or impersonal cause?

If we examine the notion that the universe had an impersonal cause we quickly run into a set of difficulties. The first difficulty is of motive or motivation. If we have an infinite self-existent entity that is impersonal (purely natural) then what brought about the motivation or motive for the universes appearance. In other words, an impersonal entity made of matter and energy has no motives, creative or otherwise. If an impersonal entity had a creative motivation it wouldn't be impersonal.

The astute reader will note that the question has only been pushed one step back. If we had a universe that needed to be explained we now have a cause that needs to be explained. If everything that exists depends upon something else for its existence then there had to be something at the start, something that began the whole process of existence itself that is itself unexplainable.

Aristotle, the famous Greek philosopher of antiquity, posited this very thing. He claimed that there must be an uncaused first cause at the beginning of the universe. He called this first cause the unmoved mover. Imagine for a moment that the universe and everything within it were a set of dominoes setup in perfect order so that when one tipped the next one in line fell. This is a picture of causation—a chain of events being set in motion by the one before. If our observation is correct, the universe is indeed like this—everything caused by another thing and so on and so forth. The problem, due to the impossibility of infinite regress, is that at some point there has to be a beginning. In other words, who tipped the first domino?

Following the Fork

This cosmic domino-tipper entity, posited by Aristotle, is the unmoved mover—the explanation for the universe. This being or entity does not owe its existence to anything else. It is self-existent. This concept of a self-existent being might remind you of God, and well it should, but we aren't even at that point yet. We are merely seeking to understand what kind of cause the universe may have had.

The important thing to note at this juncture is that whatever kind of cause we may determine to be behind the universe; it must not owe its existence to anything else. It must be a self sufficient cause, holding within itself the reason for both itself and the universe. This kind of cause would necessarily be both the foundation and boundary of all reality.

For this reason it is difficult to fully understand or comprehend the first cause. To be truthful, it is impossible. Unlike every other being or entity on the earth you cannot study it from all sides, metaphysically speaking. When we observe another person we comprehend them through the lens of our reality. In other words, *we* have an explanation or cause for our existence and so do they. As humans we interpret life as derivative beings. We have come from somewhere.

The first cause could have no cause, no history, and no point of origin. The first cause is uncaused and thus we cannot study its origin. But, we can study its originality. While the first cause may be uncaused it did indeed cause something else to exist, namely, the universe. By studying the universe itself we come upon a set of clues to what kind of cause it may have had.

As stated earlier, the universe teaches us that something never comes from nothing. So, the universe had a cause. And, the idea of an impersonal cause fails to explain the universe. What would cause raw matter and energy to transform into the universe as we know it? Positing an impersonal cause only pushes the question one step back and you still need a reason for the universe. We are left with only one possibility: that the universe had a personal cause.

Obviously, the universe exists. Having determined that it came into existence at a particular point we can surmise that this outcome was intentional. The universe didn't just happen. It happened on purpose. The universe is laden with intention, and intention is a characteristic of personality.

It is here that Christianity stakes its claim. According to Christianity the universe did indeed have a cause and that cause was personal. According to the Christian story the first cause was God, an infinitely self-existent and uncaused being. What of the impossibility of an infinite regress you may ask? If an infinite universe is impossible then wouldn't an infinite God be impossible as well? A fair question, to be sure. The answer lies in the nature of the entity.

With an eternal God, we have a being that is personal. This is the critical distinction. An impersonal self-existent universe cannot account for itself. It lacks the impetus for its own genesis or transformation. That impetus, the divine spark of existence, is a distinguishing mark of personality. There is a personality behind the universe.

In the Christian story we are presented with a reality that is not purely natural, but also supernatural. The logical difficulties that we face and the deep existential questions of life both find their answer in God, for in Him alone we have a first cause for the universe that is sufficient to account for it. In other words, God is the only being big enough to contain the universe and everything within it.

If He exists, then He was the creator of physical reality and it was He who imparted the measure of meaning into life itself. He is the reason for the universe that you and I inhabit and the reason for you and me. He is infinite but the universe He created is not. Thus, we have a finite universe with an infinite God who does not exist within it but who is instead the limit and boundary of its reality. This fits well into Aristotle's unmoved mover hypothesis in which he posited that the cause of all finite causes must be itself infinite.

We have come to a place of choosing—back to the start of the old road. We are speaking here of the boundary and beginning of reality. This is the one door that we cannot open. As spoken of earlier, we must choose something eternal, something infinite at the beginning that began everything else.

We must either choose an eternal universe with seemingly indefensible logical problems or accept an eternal personality. Both choices require faith but only one is reasonable. In fact, reason is only possible in a universe with a personality behind it. Reason has no purpose or value in a universe where it is not measured according to an authoritative external standard. In a purely physical and impersonal universe there would be no purpose in searching for a reason. There would be no such things as purpose or reason at all. These words imply an external standard by which particulars can be measured.

The very act of seeking a cause for the universe or an answer to ones existential questions—the essence of the scientific impulse—demonstrates the type of universe we live in. As real people who exist in this universe we ask questions because deep down we know the answers exist.

6

On the Road Again

Having examined the philosophical question of God's existence I feel it appropriate to continue down the path of Christianity. To be clear, I don't presume to have proved that God does indeed exist; I don't believe that it's entirely possible to do so. If the God of Christianity really does exist then it would be impossible to prove He did. It would be like trying to escape the world by falling off the edge. Reality, like the world, is a sphere, but inverted. If God exists then He is the ultimate boundary of reality.

Let us take a moment to consider a well known paradox. Skeptics and critics enjoy asking Christians what I am sure they perceive to be a wonderfully nasty question. The question is, "Can God make a rock that He can't lift?" This is often asked with a silly grin or a stupid smile...but that's beside the point.

The answer is no. The answer to that question is simple but the explanation is more complicated although the difficulty doesn't lie with the answer. It is with the question itself. For you see, the question seeks to discredit the concept of God as an omnipotent being by setting Him against Himself. The result of this is nonsense. It is a meaningless question. If God is omnipotent (all powerful) then He would be unable to make something more powerful (a rock, or anything for that matter) than Himself. He is already, by definition, an *all* powerful being. In fact, He is the most powerful. If God could make something more powerful than Himself than He wouldn't really be God at all. This would be a violation of His intrinsic nature.

So, as we examine the idea of proving God we can apply this same logic. If God really does exist we could not violate His nature as the bounds of reality. Simply put, you cannot get behind God in order to prove He exists. He is behind you and that is how you know that you exist. C.S. Lewis once said, "I believe in Christianity as I believe the sun has risen: not only because I see it, but because by it I see everything else." The idea is that God is the basis for all reality and it is only in the acceptance of Him as such that we can really see Him. Proving God outside of presupposing His existence is like trying to describe the color pink to a blind man. God's existence *is* the reference point for any discussion *of* His existence.

Thankfully, God didn't leave the matter there. If we continue our walk along the path of Christianity we will see more than could be imagined of God. We will see His nature, His character, and His name. We began this book by examining the idea that truth can be stranger than fiction, reality more fantastic than fantasy. Perhaps you have heard the Christian story about life and dismissed it as fiction. I ask that you would open your eyes once more to take another look. Perhaps what you dismissed as a fairy tale was the truth. Perhaps your eyes were clouded with the dust of your own journey through life. What we have *seen* often influences what we can *see*.

That so, truth and reality are not matters of perception. Truth is that which describes a real state of affairs and Christianity claims to be nothing less than absolute truth. Christianity is less a religion than it is a statement about reality itself. If Christianity is a story it is everyone's story, the story of history and of the future alike. If it is true, it is not true for some and false for others.

Christianity may tell a fantastic story but it is not a fiction. If it were, it would not be written as it is, for it appeals not to the heart of man but the heart of heaven. It isn't the story of man's struggle and eventual triumph. It is the story of his failure and fall seen from the loving eyes of His maker. It is the tale of betrayal met with mercy and darkness met with light. It is the story of God becoming a man so He could overcome evil with good. Christianity is not a child's tale even though you must become like a child to truly receive it. The Christian story is full of pain but it promises unimaginable pleasure. It is not for the weak of heart.

We stepped off the path of Christianity after discussing the fall of man at Eden. That battle was only the first of many but if you listen closely you can still hear the echo of it in your heart, for it was in that moment that our hearts were torn asunder. You and I were broken then, though we may not recognize it. It was at that battle that we were cut off from the source of our significance and the measure of our meaning. We didn't just lose a battle, we lost ourselves. And since that time we have been looking for something to heal us. We are empty vessels who long to be filled.

Have you ever looked at the world around you and wondered, "Why is there so much pain and evil?" Even on the happiest and sunniest days we know in the back of our minds that someone somewhere is living a nightmare. Maybe that person is you. What of this? We know that something is wrong with our world. There are a thousand different prescriptions for the problems that plague our world but none seem to work. The problems of pain and evil are not surface wounds. Those problems are as deep as the heart.

And it is the heart of man, your heart and mine that God looks to heal. Many people observe, or even try, Christianity for a short while but then turn away from it, their symptoms unhealed. They have missed the point. The Christian faith provides a total transformation from the heart outwards. You don't give a man with a failing heart a bandage. He needs a new heart. The symptoms of evil in ourselves and in our world cannot be healed with ideological bandages.

The Christian prescription is at once more difficult than any other because it doesn't promise a fast and easy fix. To become a Christian is to give your entire life to Christ as both Lord and Savior. We must strive to rid ourselves of the thought that Christianity is something we can add to our life instead of something we trade our life for. The question that arises is immediately pragmatic: Is it worth it? Two things must guide our thinking along this line. First, what do you receive when you become a Christian? Second, what if you don't?

I'll answer the second question first. What happens if you refuse Christ? Simply put, He honors your choice. You are left to fend for yourself. If you refuse His aid and fellowship you get what you asked for, His absence. The problem with this outcome is that you and I were made *by* Him and *for* Him. If the Christian story is the true story of God's redemptive working through history than we will never be whole apart from Him.

As for the first question, it has a simple answer. When you become a Christian you trade your life for the life of Jesus Christ. In Christian theology this has deep significance because Jesus' life isn't like yours or mine. His life was sinless, perfect, and holy. His life is eternal. His life is acceptable in the sight of God. Ours on the other hand is not. We are deeply flawed individuals. But I may be getting ahead of myself because the best way to truly understand the Christian answer to the human predicament is to clearly see the problem.

The fall of man, discussed in a previous chapter, is central to the Christian understanding of man's predicament. As is implied by the term 'fall,' Christians believe that the state of the current world is not what God originally intended it to be. God created mankind for significant relationship and that was only possible through the gift of choice. God's desire to give love to and to be loved by man was only possible with the contingency of significant free will. This is perhaps one of the deepest mysteries of God's character; that He of infinite wisdom and perfect foreknowledge would choose to create significantly free beings in light of their foreseen failure.

Now, it should be noted that Christians have differing opinions on the matter of free will and sovereignty but for our purposes it is enough to know that God indeed felt it more valuable to create man than not to. What emerges as one studies the Christian faith is the beautiful love story of a God who not only gave life *to* man because of love but who also gave His life *for* man because of love. God in His infinite wisdom and foreknowledge anticipated the failure of His beloved and provided a way of reconciliation. But again, I get ahead of myself. What of the fall?

What really happened at the fall? Adam, the gatekeeper, let in the wolf. The fall wasn't just a metaphor for man's frailty; it was a real event with real consequences. We were severed from life, from love, and from hope. We were separated from God.

Christianity paints this bleak picture of man's condition; one more reason it isn't anything like a man-made religion. Christianity defies human understanding because it places the hope for our salvation impossibly beyond our grasp. We are not the heroes in the Christian story, God is.

And what heroic action did God undertake but the salvation of an entire race—the human race, past, present, and future. To truly understand this heroism we must see man's predicament in its fullness. The light and beauty of God's grace can only be fully seen in its contrast with the blackness of sin.

What is this stain upon our soul? It is the mark of pride and rebellion. In the garden mankind made a choice to oppose the authority of God and in so doing allowed evil to enter his own heart. The problems we face in the world are not as external as we might think. They find their origin in us, in our rebellion against God.

In Christian theology the Fall was the entrance of sin into the equation of man's relationship with God. God created man with a significantly free will and man chose to exercise his will in disobedience. Adam attempted to usurp the authority of divinity but inherited death. This death, this darkness, is what stains our souls. It is the source of war and the wasting of human life. It is the source of evil. It is the enemy within us.

This enemy is at once more insidious and dangerous than many others because it dwells within. It cannot be fought with any weapons of human origin. It cannot be medicated, psychoanalyzed, or even exorcised. Like a parasite that has so entwined itself into its host that to destroy it is to destroy one's self, sin has a hold on us.

The only escape that is offered is death. To kill the beast you must die. This conjures up a rather macabre image but it's true. The parasite of evil feeds on the human heart and will live as long as its host. And so to be free one must die. This shouldn't surprise us, the twisted nature of evil as it is. Are we so naïve that we cannot see the reality of evil? Why should real evil not have a real cost. Perhaps it is the cost we find too steep: life and death. But life and death are often laid on the line in our human experience.

When we engage in our basest desires the result is often a matter of life and death. Murderers steal the breath from their victims. Warlords send children into battle to fight for their greed. The powerful of this world often crush the weak and poor. Evil doesn't play by the rules. Or rather, evil plays by the rules but always breaks them. To put it simply, evil leads to death wherever it is found. So why should we be surprised that death is introduced when we find evil in our hearts?

If one would be free from this burdensome weight they must die. The problem with this line of reasoning is that it's rather impossible to enjoy life when you are dead. And so we face a conundrum of gigantic proportions. If I am to be free from the evil within me I must die; but if I die I cannot enjoy my freedom. Sadly, the problem is actually even more complex than I make it.

Even if I were to die for my own sins, the evil in my own heart, I still wouldn't be free. I still wouldn't be fulfilled. I still wouldn't be made right. The problem with evil is that it isn't just a passive entity. Evil isn't just a parasite we've allowed to exist within us. It is something that we've embraced and it's something that we have engaged in. Hard as it is to admit, we have committed evil and in so doing have committed treason against God and even ourselves.

You and I were made to exist in relationship with God—an absolutely perfect being. When God created us we were also perfect and that perfection is what we lost at the Fall. Now, to be restored to our rightful place we find that perfection is the required price. If I am to dwell in the light of a perfect God there can be no spot on my soul be it great or small. There can be no shadow or stain.

And here we begin to see the great depths of our predicament. We, the fallen, have been cut off from our only hope of joy, our only hope of peace, and our only chance of fulfillment. Even if our death could pay the price of our mistakes it couldn't pay the price of perfection. It is one thing to pay for crimes committed and quite another to have never done them.

This is where we stand. Death itself wouldn't be enough to set us right. The chasm that stretches before us is impossible to cross. The person who has committed evil, even just once, cannot claim perfection and consequently cannot be permitted to stand in the presence of God. Perhaps you find fault with a God who would shun imperfection? I ask you to consider the possibility that we in our imperfection are not excluded for God's benefit but for our own.

There is something to be feared in perfection for the imperfect. You and I couldn't survive the presence of perfection. Our imperfections would burn through us like dross out of precious metal in the refiner's fire. We would be destroyed in the presence of God and yet it is only in His presence that we can be whole. This is both our greatest yearning—to be one with Him again—and our greatest dilemma.

We feel our separation in a thousand different ways and we long for perfection. Perfection is that state in which there is no separation, no cracks or fissures. It is that moment where everything has its rightful place and nothing is out of order. In perfection there is no anger, hate, or fear. In perfection there is no distance between those that love each other. It is often said there are no perfect people but if we are to stand in the presence of God nothing less than perfection will do.

7

Perfection's Path

Christianity takes an interesting turn at this point. Perhaps you are rolling your eyes as you read these words in anticipation of my eventual attempt to 'give you religion' or something of that nature but I beg your attention for a few moments longer. I can't give you anything. I can't give you faith or doubt or anything in-between. This path is yours to walk alone. Your path from this point is only wide enough for one.

This path is one we all must tread without our friends, family, or even our enemies. Our only companions on this portion of the road are our failures and our faith. Earlier I spoke of courage and conviction. If you posses them then call them to your side. I will pose just one question as you stand ready to proceed. Are you perfect?

Before you answer that question consider what we've already determined. Perfection is the price to stand in the presence of God and His presence is your only hope of fulfillment. So the question is: what will you do now? Will you hold up your deeds to be judged? Will you beg for mercy? Will you stride boldly into heaven's throne room and demand your dues? What will you do?

How will you navigate perfection's path? This question is what compels us down the road of Christianity. The Christian story has been a terrible one indeed up to now. It has tugged at our hearts with glimpses of what once was and shown us the inadequacy of even our own death to solve our crisis but the most terrible moment still approaches—the moment of decision.

As stated earlier, when it comes to the really important questions of life neutrality isn't an option. The appearance of neutrality when it comes to the matter of faith is merely an illusion. The man who says that he has no conviction either way concerning Christ has just clearly stated his conviction. To be unconvinced or uncommitted is to be *something*— pitiful as that *something* may be. We are all racing towards eternity or oblivion at breakneck speed and the man who pretends to be watching the rest of us go by as he sits on the curb is a fool.

And so, if we are to be realistic about life we must answer the question: Am I perfect? Knowing all the pregnant promises that perfection holds I cringe at answering in the negative but to answer yes makes me a liar. For I know that I have done wrong, in my own case repeatedly so; in yours I cannot speak. But for myself I must answer the question honestly and that places me among the ranks of the fallen ones, the imperfect, the sinners and the scoundrels. I stand with murderers, liars, and thieves.

I have no excuse before God. He is the standard of perfection and anything less than perfection denies me access. I cannot point to my neighbor and say, "I'm not as bad as him." He is not the standard. The comparison is not made in shades of gray but rather between black and white. Because I am imperfect I stand on this side of the line in rank with the best and worst of the imperfect. If a hundred men set off to swim across a lake and then all drown it is irrelevant who got closest to shore. And so it is with perfection.

There is no such thing as almost perfect. Perfection has a definite edge. This hard truth allows us to put away talk of moral relativism. Even the man whose morals are like water needs something to hold them in lest they escape his grasp. The man who owns to no standard has established a standard that he will be judged by. In this case, even if you aim at the wrong target it can still be determined if you missed. No person can claim perfection even if their standard differs from God's.

There is no perfect Christian, Jew, or Muslim. All have fallen short of God's glory even if some have fallen shorter. It is of no use to take pride in one's understanding of truth or diligent adherence to a certain creed for this reason. We've all lost perfection's path.

And here we turn to the great claim of the Christian faith: that someone found perfection's path and followed it. And what's more, offered to lead us down the path. This revelation may not seem overtly groundbreaking but let me elaborate. We've seen that no one has ever attained perfection. No person has ever achieved that standard. So the proclamation that someone indeed did should be of particular interest to us.

Imagine that you were standing in a crowd of people on the street when someone suddenly leapt into the air and started to fly around. The awe and wonder that would arise would be immediate. Humans can't fly. For all of known human history we have been a grounded bunch. Our amazement would have a certain quality to it though. Our wonder wouldn't be for the act of flight itself. We've seen birds fly and even achieved flight aided by machines. The real wonder would be for someone's doing something that no other person had ever done before. They would be totally unique, wholly separated from the rest of us. It would be for this reason that our attention would be drawn to them like a moth to the flame.

An event of this magnitude did indeed take place in history. Someone emerged from the crowd and did something that no one had ever done before; something that nobody even imagined was possible—

demonstrated perfection. So we approach our moment of decision. A choice is offered to us: take your own path in pursuit of perfection or follow someone else; but not just anyone else, someone who already walked perfection's path. The Christian faith presents its namesake as this person. Jesus Christ is the one who tread perfection's path. He lived a perfect life, died upon a Roman cross, and was raised from the dead by God.

It is this proclamation which separates the Christian faith from all the rest. To be a Christian is not to try and achieve perfection through your own wisdom, obedience, and sacrifice. It is to stop trying to do those things and allow them to be done on your behalf. The Christian ideal is not that we can do something for ourselves. It is rather the declaration that we cannot. The bad news comes before the good. Man is completely and irreparably separated from the God who dwells at the end of perfection's path.

The good news comes in when we see this man Jesus, the one who bids us to follow Him down perfection's path and to come and die. What a strange being He is. I profess to be a Christian but I do not profess to fully understand Christ. He is unique in every way. He thinks, speaks, and acts differently than I do but He is the one who walked perfection's path and so I follow.

8

The Perfect Man

Perhaps you are familiar with Jesus. You may have heard the Christian claim that He died for the sins of mankind and rose from the dead. Perhaps you know Him as a prophet or a teacher or even as someone you can pray to. These things all have their rightful place but I wish to take you further back into His story and examine what makes Him so special. What significance should the death of Christ or His resurrection have to you?

Perfection's path didn't begin in Gethsemane. It wasn't the Via Dolorosa. It stretched back longer, all the way from Bethlehem to Golgotha via Nazareth and Galilee. Perfection's path wasn't trod in a night. It took a lifetime to complete. Jesus' steps from Gethsemane to Golgotha were merely the closing notes of a symphony, each step the triumphant exclamation of a hundred-thousand perfect steps that had brought him to that place. The crucifixion and resurrection of Jesus are crucial moments within the

Christian story but they depend upon the perfect life that Jesus lived. Christ's crucifixion would have had no more significance than the death of the criminals to His right and left had it not been for His perfection.

As we have previously discussed, no person has ever walked perfection's path. No person of any faith or creed has laid claim to that achievement except one. But it is to perfection that Christ lays claim, with no lack of confidence and no question of right. As others have noted at length, to make this claim one must either be crazy or correct.

We shouldn't fear the bold men who make a few great proclamations. Their claims are easily sorted out. It is the timid men who live in the twilight and make thousands of impossibly small claims that we should fear. Lies hide in the multitude of words. They hide in the shadows of qualification. Strange as it may ultimately be found to be, the truth always dwells in the light. It doesn't hide. The man who claims He is God can quickly be cast down or lifted up.

The Perfect Man

And so with Jesus we have a choice to make. He made some of the boldest claims ever heard upon the earth and we must face them. Who is Jesus? This question is the central issue of the Christian faith. Jesus himself asked His disciples this question and He is asking it of us, "Who am I to you?" If He is who He says He is then we must take great care with Him.

Christ has been called many things: a prophet, a revolutionary, a teacher, and even a paradox, but when He referred to Himself He often used the title "Son of Man." Jesus often emphasized his fraternity with mankind and expressed His solidarity with our predicament. When we examine Him and see His divinity the tendency is to diminish his humanity but He was fully human. Christ didn't become less human because He was also God. He was in fact more human than even we are.

Imagine a shirt which has been abused and soiled and finally cut into rags to serve base purposes around the household. Now lay that pile of rags next to a brand new shirt and tell me which one better represents its original design. Here we have a picture of Christ's humanity contrasted with our own. We are men cut to ribbons while He is perfect. He was not a super-man but rather a man as men were meant to be.

Jesus has been called the second Adam because they were the only ones who enjoyed the perfection of being men as God intended men to be. The difference between them was that Adam walked in sinless, unspoiled perfection in the Garden of Eden and fell down whereas Jesus walked in sinless, unspoiled perfection amongst the squalor of humanity and raised us up.

But Jesus isn't only the Son of Man. He is also the Son of God. And this distinction is of great importance. Jesus isn't a mere man. He is also divine. He is the Son, the second person of the Trinity, co-equal with the Father and Holy Spirit as the great creeds declare. Jesus is Immanuel, God with us. His coming was God's response to our great need.

We, the fallen ones, the hopelessly lost, are incapable of pulling ourselves out of the pit. God in His wisdom and mercy humbled Himself to walk among us as a man for only a man could walk perfection's path for other men to follow and only God is perfect. And so we have the Christian claim that Jesus was fully God and fully man, the promised Messiah of Israel and the world.

Jesus lived a perfect life of obedience to God and then offered Himself willingly as the payment for our sins and the pattern of our perfection. When we see the significance of what Jesus did at the cross we mustn't stop at His payment of sins. As we have seen earlier, our own death wouldn't satisfy the debt we owe. Death doesn't achieve perfection. The wages of sin is death. Sin leads to death but death doesn't lead to perfection or eternal life. Perfection is the requirement to enter heaven and the presence of God.

So the full significance of what Christ accomplished is only seen when we understand both God's mercy *and* grace at work in Christ. Mercy is the forgiveness of sins while grace is the gift of righteousness. Jesus' death satisfied the deficit of evil but His life provided the requirement of perfection. Christ becomes the pivot point of our faith or our doubt. What we will we do with Him? He bids us to come but we may stay. He bids us to follow but we have the freedom to flee. He offers us His life but we may keep our own if that is what we wish.

What is vital to understand is that our choice at this moment is of incredible importance to our eternal future. Whatever our choice may be it has real consequences. I may reject Christ but I am consequently choosing something else. To make this clearer let it be said that Jesus isn't one out of a hundred essentially equal options. Every choice is a yes or no, an acceptance or a rejection. You cannot take just a little of Jesus and leave the rest.

As I conclude this chapter I think it important to note that the choice we all face is not a complicated one. Though the world is bursting at the seams with religions, philosophies, and worldviews the choice can be whittled down to just two. It is a choice between Christianity and everything-else. You see, Jesus Christ makes a very exclusive claim in John 14:6 where He claims to be, "the way, the truth, and the life" and the *only* way to the Father. There is no shallow end of the pool in Christianity where you can just 'get your feet wet,' and anyone who tells you otherwise is sorely mistaken. It's a total commitment. There is no messing about with Christ and Buddha or Christ and Hedonism. If you have a little of something else, you have none of Christ, and worse yet, He has none of you.

9

Difficult Ground

Having examined who Jesus is we have encountered several perplexing questions that need to be dealt with. As on any path there is difficult ground. One of the more difficult patches that men have identified has to do with God's becoming a man in the person of Jesus Christ.

The question of God's becoming a man in Jesus—what theology has called the Incarnation—has often been called a paradox and has often been challenged as such. But why should its being a paradox have anything to do with it's being a reality? Many of the most commonly accepted realities are every bit as paradoxical. It all has to do with asking the question: why should *this* be the case rather than *that*?

Why should the elephant be large rather than small? Why should he have great big ears and a small tail instead of the other way round? I pose the question: what makes him an elephant at all? What is his essential quality of elephant-ishness that makes him instantly recognizable to us all?

You could say that his physical attributes make him an elephant and you'd be right in one way but wrong in another. His physical appearance makes him recognizable but it doesn't define him. Would he cease to be an elephant if he lost his trunk and tail? No. He wouldn't be a mouse if he had no tail just as a man wouldn't be a monkey if he did. Attributes alone, physical or otherwise, don't give us the full equation. There is something wholly other which describes and identifies things. There is an *idea* of each thing which makes it what it is.

According to Christianity each thing has its place and is itself because it is a creation of the mind of God. This is why an elephant without a trunk is still an elephant and a man without a hand still a man. This almost indescribable quality which identifies things as they are and as unique from others can only be spoken of analogously. So when we talk about the elephant we talk about his trunk and large ears but we understand that there is something more to him which makes him what he is.

There is something behind the curtains, if you will, that informs existence. It can't be felt or seen but it can be recognized. It is like the light which reveals the subtle intricacies of a great painting. The colors emerge to be studied only because something has infused them with their character. Vision is not possible without light and so it is with the God of the universe. We could not see reality if there were no light cast upon it from beyond. God imagines and we discover.

When we talk of difficult ground we must understand that it is with relative terms. Something is only as difficult as I am unable to accomplish it. The garden fence may be the Great Wall of China to an infant but to a grown man a trifling obstacle. It is not the object but the observer which assigns the difficulty. And so it is with God. The obstacle which may appear to be insurmountable to a mere man is but a garden fence to the Almighty. The difficulty of every problem depends upon the perspective one has of it.

And so it is with the Incarnation of Christ. We must ask the question: "Why should God accomplish His mission into humanity another way instead of the way He did?" This idea, of God becoming a man, is often too great an obstacle for people to overcome, but why? If the God of the bible really exists could He not accomplish such a thing? Again, perhaps it is not His ability to perform a seemingly paradoxical action that is questionable but rather our ability to comprehend it.

It is much the same with other supernatural events spoken of in the scriptures. Take your pick from: the Red Sea crossing, fire from heaven, manna, Lazarus being raised from the dead, etc. There are hundreds of miracles recorded in the scriptures that are seemingly impossible. But if we accept that our world is more than just an amalgamation of purposeless matter and that perhaps personal forces are at work behind the scenes; even the most unlikely things can take their rightful place. It is a matter of perspective. The universe looks much different in the light of God's existence. This is why it has often been said that if a man could accept the first four words of the bible, "In the beginning God," than they could accept the rest of it.

Another problem with the line of reasoning that would deny the veracity of the Christian faith based on its seeming paradoxes is that every worldview has paradox. Paradox and difficulty are found within all worldviews. Thus, paradox and difficulty cannot be used as the ultimate and infallible standards. I cannot affirm my own worldview and deny another based on mere improbability. If life demonstrates anything it is that truth is often stranger than fiction. The reality that the Christian faith claims is totally fantastic but it is not a fantasy. There are many events in my own history that I wouldn't believe had really happened if someone had to convince me they did.

Imagine a scenario in which you hit your head and lost your memory. You awake in a hospital bed with people around you claiming to be your friends and loved ones. As it becomes clear that you do not remember the events of your life they begin to inform you of them.

You are told where you got that scar on your cheek, who you've loved and lost, what jobs you've had, and all the rest. Some of the information makes sense but some of it seems totally improbable. You just can't believe that you flipped a car six times when you were sixteen or ever played in a jazz band. This situation would be difficult for any of us to go through; to have to accept on authority the events of our own life. And yet, this is an accurate picture of reality for all of us. So much of what we *know* in life is based on the witness and authority of others.

In our imagined scenario we trusted that even the most improbable events recounted to us were accurate because the people were trustworthy. If we knew that the people telling us our life story loved us and had our best interest in mind we would be infinitely more inclined to accept what they said. And so it becomes more a question of *who* is telling us rather than *what* they are telling us. So it is with life. We accept things as truth based on how probable they are to our reason while simultaneously accepting unreasonable things based on our personal experience of them or the reliability and trustworthiness of other witnesses.

In life we accept unusual events and circumstances rather routinely depending upon their presentation to us. Crazy things happen to us and we accept them because we experienced them to be real, no matter how unusual they may have been. Or, we accept that an event that we would be predisposed to disbelieve in really did occur because someone we trust insisted it did. So this difficulty with the Incarnation and other supernatural or paradoxical things found in the Christian story must be cast in proper light. They are only difficulties for the man who doesn't believe in God.

This is not to say that they are commonplace or normal to the Christian. They are miracles no matter how you view them. It is simply to say that the Christian feels warranted in accepting the Incarnation and other supernatural events in the Christian story because of their belief in God and their personal experience of them.

This might sound a little naive, and perhaps it is, but the problem is really simpler than most make it out to be. The miraculous events recorded in the bible either happened or they did not. Determining the probability of their occurrence falls to the kind of universe one accepts as a presupposition. In a universe created by God they are exceedingly plausible. In a universe with no God they are as impossible as a square circle. This is why the real debate is not a matter of probability but rather of presupposition. It all comes back to one's fundamental views of reality and truth.

If we disagree on the fundamental nature of reality we cannot have a reasonable discussion about the probability of the Incarnation or the supernatural. It would be like having two sports teams compete on the same field while each adhered to a different set of rules. Actually it would be like the teams playing two totally different games. The local basketball team cannot claim victory over the baseball team because they scored more points. They are in two separate spheres which have no logical interaction. I cannot tell you that four plus four equals eight because William the Conqueror won the battle of Hastings. William won the battle but it is irrelevant to the mathematical equation in question.

To be clear, I am not discouraging the pursuit of truth when it comes to the supernatural. I am merely pointing out the absurdity involved in trying to discount the probability of the supernatural when one denies its very possibility. If one denies God's existence then what is the point of trying to cast doubt on anything that logically comes after Him.

The person who denies God and then seeks to disprove the supernatural is like a man who hunts for an imaginary creature's eggs. I don't give much attention to the things I don't believe exist. I don't search for the Easter Bunny or wait up on Christmas Eve for Santa Claus. But I also don't shout aloud that the present-bearing fat man in red is a myth when he doesn't emerge from out of the fireplace. I just eat the cookies.

To change direction a little let me just say that I don't blindly accept all accounts of the supernatural. In fact, I doubt most of them. The reason for this is because I genuinely believe in their reality and possibility. Being someone who accepts the possibility of the miraculous because I believe in God gives me perspective with regards to degrees of the supernatural. Some reported miracles are just that, divine interactions between heaven and earth, others are not. The shades of plausibility and probability are revealed only to the person whose eyes are aided by the light of an infinite-personal God.

10

The Narrow Road

In the last chapter we covered some difficult ground but now we come to the most difficult ground of all. It is at this point on the path that the road to life grows narrow and we are told that few find it. I believe the reason that few find the road that leads to life has nothing to do with how hard it is to discover but rather how hard it is to travel. I am aware of more great challenges in the world than I have personally undertaken. There is a great gulf between knowledge and action and nowhere is this gulf wider than when it comes to making a decision about God.

Oh, we may accept that *a* God is there or that every person can have their own private god, higher power, spiritual master, etc. but this ultimately denies *the* God of heaven and earth. We have found that we need not deny ultimate power, only its exclusivity. We want a spiritual democracy, not a Sovereign.

Relativism, the view that opposing and exclusive beliefs can both be true, ultimately destroys *all* beliefs. If *all* mutually exclusive truth claims can be true then none of them are. We cannot adopt this position because it is self defeating. The very instant an individual accepts relativism as truth they deny its veracity.

In the last chapter I spoke of the simplicity of the problem; it's black and white nature. It greatly depends upon one's presuppositions but it ultimately boils down to a choice between Christianity and everything-else. I believe that the choice is indeed limited to these two options based on the simple fact that Christianity presents itself as *exclusive* truth. This means that either Christianity is true or that it is not. There is no middle ground. Now to the relativistic mind of today, where 'truth' is not a category, my statement is quite problematic. I imagine that I would be considered 'dogmatic' and 'intolerant' in the worst way possible.

And here we come to one of the first divisions that Orthodox Christianity brings. To be an

Orthodox Christian you can't be a relativist in the area of truth. You must view truth in the same way that the Christian God views truth. In other words, you must view truth as a category. This means that some things are true and that others are un-true. If Christianity is in fact true, then every other religion or worldview is un-true. It's like an old-western movie where a gunslinger walks into the saloon, looks across the room at his rival, and utters the timeless challenge, "This town ain't big enough fer the both of us."

Christianity makes that same challenge. But in this case it is something more serious than a Texas turf war at stake. This battle is over the subject of truth. Oh and by the way, neutrality isn't an option. You see, whether or not you choose to accept the *Christian* claim to truth you must choose *something* to accept. When you deny something you are in fact replacing it with something else. If you deny the existence of something then you are in the same moment affirming the opposite as true. This cannot be avoided. Belief is a space that is always full. As Thoreau said, "Nature abhors a vacuum…"

The 'truth question' *is* being answered by everyone at all times whether they are aware of it or not. You believe in *something* even if what you believe in is *nothing*. To believe in nothing is the belief that all other beliefs are false. You cannot escape an affirmation.

What do you affirm and subsequently deny about God, the universe, and yourself? What do you believe and can you support it? Many people simply go through life 'seeing' things a certain way without ever thinking about it. What separates Christians, atheists, and the rest isn't *what* they see but rather *how* they see it. Christians, Atheists, Buddhists, Hindus, and Muslims all see pain and pleasure in the world. We *all* experience the heights of joy contrasted with the depths of despair. We *all* see the colors of the universe, bright and dismal alike, splayed upon the canvas of life. The difference lies not in what is beheld, but in the beholders.

What I speak of here is your worldview. How do you interpret the data of life in all its complexity? By what standards do you judge reality? I, for instance, use the Bible. The Bible gives universal principles by which all particulars can be judged in the areas of truth and morality. I interpret the data of life differently than an atheist does because I have a different worldview. I see creation and he sees random chance. I see morality and he sees social convention...and so on and so forth. But putting *how* we see (our respective worldviews that is) aside for the moment, let us look at *what* we see. What is the nature of reality that we all observe?

The Orthodox Christian view of reality, which I am primarily concerned with here, is distinctive. It is a view that upholds what we call objective reality. It is the view that things are either *true* or *untrue* irrespective of how I feel about them. This is the nature of reality in science, philosophy, theology, morality, etc.

Take science for example. In the area of science there are certain realities, principles, and laws that are in constant operation. This principle can be illustrated by imagining a bicycle accident. If I run into a brick wall on a bicycle my forward motion will be suddenly and severely arrested (painfully I might add from personal experience). The wall will impede my motion because it, I, and my bicycle all have set physical properties or realities that are in operation. This is an objective scientific reality. It doesn't matter whether I like the wall, or believe in the wall, or tremendously enjoy biking in the city. The reality of bike/human versus wall is always in effect.

This type of objective scientific reality is seldom denied. The problem for most people comes when you begin to speak about objective reality in the areas of truth and morality. But why shouldn't there be discoverable truths in the areas of truth and morality?

Maybe at this point you are wondering why I am spending such a great deal of time trying to establish the existence of objective truth and reality. Sadly, there is a battle being fought over the nature of reality and it isn't just being fought between secularists and Christians. This battle is in fact being waged on two fronts and it is for this reason that I must establish my rear-guard. It does seem silly to have to battle an opponent who denies not only the validity of my position but also the validity of the battlefield itself. And yet, this *is* the nature of the conflict that Orthodox Christians face. We are forced by the postmodernist within and without the Church to establish a basis for reality.

As stated earlier, the Christian view of reality starts with a God who is self-existent and uncreated. The Christian view of reality is that there is objective truth in the natural world because it was created that way by God. God established the laws of nature and it is He that maintains them. Is it then a stretch to believe that God established the laws of truth and morality as well? In other words, why should objective truth be only limited to nature? The Christian view of reality is of an objective standard that governs *every* area of life.

Objective reality is the line in the sand that divides the true from the untrue. This belief in objective reality is really quite fundamental to the Christian position. The existence of objective reality leads us to the point where we must figure out how to determine what is true in the world. If there are *truths* in the universe, natural and spiritual alike, then I as an individual am either correctly or incorrectly relating to them. This is where the Christian worldview comes into play.

As a Christian I believe that my worldview is correct and that I can accurately see the *truths* in the universe. I believe that every other worldview gives an incorrect picture of reality. The existence of reality or, 'something to see,' is not in question here. What *is* in question is the viewer's ability to see it correctly.

Let me give an illustration. When I was a teenager (either 14 or 15 years of age) my mother brought me to an optometrist for an eye exam. It was discovered during the course of the exam that my vision was flawed and I was given a prescription for glasses. The moment I put my glasses on for the first time was a spectacular one. For the very first time I was treated to an accurate picture of the world. I will always remember that wonderful feeling of seeing clearly.

Now, what changed when I put those glasses on? The world didn't change at all. I was simply able to view the world through lenses that gave me an accurate picture of what had always been there. As time went on and my eyes adjusted I required new prescriptions so I could continue to see clearly. Finally, I opted for laser surgery to correct my eyes and bypass the glasses altogether. This is the Christian view of reality. We require a correction of our worldview to see the world as it *really is*. There are truths in science, philosophy, religion, etc, but we cannot accurately perceive them with uncorrected eyes.

So the question becomes one of deciding upon a worldview. How will you determine which one is best? I have already declared my allegiance to the Christian worldview. I believe that Christianity gives the *only* accurate view of you, me, and the universe. My Christian faith is the basis for everything I do. Its values give my life value and my existence significance. It is the universal that gives the particulars of my life clarity. But what will you choose?

It is now that we turn our attention to a comparison of worldviews. This is the part where many people disconnect from a discussion of religion. In our relativistic/pluralistic day and age, belief has been given untouchable status. If you or I question the legitimacy of another's beliefs we are guilty of intolerance (the absolute worst sin in today's society). I would like to ask the accuser where they get their notion of why this is *wrong,* but we can deal with that later.

The fact is that if I make a judgment about the objective truth or un-truth of a worldview I tread upon thin ice. If I am perceived to be intolerant I might be criticized, ostracized, or just plain disliked, but I press on. I believe that the 'truth question' is one of the most important questions anyone will ever answer. As a Christian I believe that your answer to the 'truth question' has eternal ramifications. I can't sit idly-by and not give fair warning to individuals who are in grave danger.

So what is this danger? Every individual is already answering the 'truth question.' The problem is that many are getting it wrong. Sorry to have to tread upon your self-esteem but I would rather save your soul. Will you choose to follow the narrow road?

Many people are getting the answer to the truth question wrong. And as I said earlier, this has eternal ramifications, namely, hell. The Christian view is that those people who refuse Jesus Christ as Lord and Savior will be given their desire. As C. S. Lewis once said, "There are only two kinds of people in the end: those who say to God, 'Thy will be done,' and those to whom God says, in the end, 'Thy will be done'." The danger that I speak of here is the danger that every person faces: an eternity of separation from God. This is why I don't care if I am labeled as intolerant. I am *extremely* intolerant of people going to hell.

11

Love and Tolerance

This discussion of tolerance must first be defined to avoid confusion. I see a distinct difference between true tolerance as advocated in Christianity and the twisted definition of today's society. You see, society's definition of tolerance is that nobody should ever challenge or question another's beliefs. We should all just get along and play nicely in the sandbox. This kind of tolerance is blind in that it has no standards. Anything goes.

The problem with this concept is that the word tolerance inherently carries the idea of disagreement. I don't tolerate the people I agree with, I agree with them. I can only tolerate someone I disagree with. So when you tolerate people with whom you disagree you are simply putting on apathy, thus weakening your own beliefs. You are in fact saying to the person you are supposedly tolerating, "I reject your beliefs. They are wrong. I just won't do anything about it." The Christian definition of tolerance is quite different.

The Christian ideal of tolerance is first mitigated by a higher ideal, the highest ideal in fact, the Christian ideal of love. Love in the Christian sense is the self-sacrificing motivation towards others. Jesus said in John 15:13, "Greater love has no one than this, than to lay down one's life for his friends." Jesus Christ exemplified this kind of love when He laid down His own life for the world on the cross. And now we can start to observe the contrast between tolerance without standards or truth and tolerance with love.

Christianity, as discussed earlier, upholds objective truth. I cannot, as a Christian, affirm that which I know to be false. In this sense I cannot tolerate the beliefs of others that are at odds with Christian standards. But I can do one better. I can love people. Love is so much stronger than tolerance. True Christian tolerance is not to apathetically stand and watch as people believe in lies on their way to hell. It is to challenge their error with truth in a loving way so as to bring about the greater good in the individual. This process can be uncomfortable and even painful, but it is far superior to tolerance without standards.

Tolerance, in the modern sense, is to say, "I will do nothing to harm you, but I will also do nothing to keep you from harm." Imagine two men standing near a sea-cliff. If one of the men suddenly became convinced that he could fly and decided to leap from the cliff, would it not be better for his friend to grab hold of him and attempt to dissuade him from his purpose rather than let him jump? What if the man who was convinced he could fly begged and pleaded to be released so that he could take flight? What if he began to violently attack his friend who was holding him? Would it be right for the man who was trying to save his friend to push him down and sit upon him until help arrived? This might cause the deluded man pain and discomfort. "Well," you say, "he is obviously un-well and needs to be restrained for his own good!" Yes, and this is the position Christians often find themselves in, holding people back from the cliff!

The man who was in his right mind would not be guilty of any crime if his friend just leapt off a cliff because of a delusion. He didn't push him or trick him into thinking he could fly. He would have no *legal* responsibility to save his friend, and yet, he would have a *moral* one.

This is just an example of where tolerance without standards can go horribly wrong. The Christian standard is to love people enough to let them experience the pain that leads to their good. If I go to the doctor and he discovers cancer in my body, I don't want him to smile and say everything's fine just to make me feel good. I want to know the negative news so we can work on a hopefully positive outcome. Get me into chemo therapy and on the medicine I need even though it will hurt. In other words, give me the pain now so I can fight for my life.

As a Christian, honestly adhering to my beliefs, it would be wrong for me to simply tolerate people. To tolerate someone is to hold them at arm's length and allow them to come no further. It is to maintain that barrier of calloused indifference so common in the world today.

Love and Tolerance

Loneliness is at an all-time high in the world today despite our great technological advances in communication. Why is this so? It is because modern people have become as plastic as their technology in their views of God, truth, and morality. In a world where everything goes, nothing is holy, nothing is real, and nothing is true. Tolerance is the perpetual existence of unopposed error. But I don't tolerate this state of affairs.

My Christianity compels me to love my fellow man. This is where true Christian tolerance comes into the picture. I can disagree with the worldviews of others and yet I do not keep them at arm's length. I do not simply ignore them or treat them with apathy. I can disagree with them and yet show them love. I can speak the *truth* to them, but with love. This concept comes from the heart of God Himself, that Truth and Love are inseparable. When one loses the other it ceases to be something that is helpful.

Love without Truth is self-serving in that it seeks the pleasure of the giver over the good of the recipient. It's like the doctor trying to save me from pain by not telling me about my cancer. Really, this kind of love is for the benefit of the giver and it actually hurts more than it helps.

This is the kind of *love* seen in tolerance without truth. It is the *affection* that will not challenge, and so allows *infection* to continue. Is it more loving to let someone who is addicted to heroin continue in their addiction unchallenged, or to intervene? If a father sees his son playing with a poisonous serpent in the lawn would not the greatest love be to pull the boy away, even if it caused the boy pain? The father could have avoided causing his son's anguish at losing his new found pet by not intervening, but then what?

When I was a child, I would have delighted to have had ice-cream for dinner and candy for breakfast. I would have rather watched Scooby-Doo than gone to the First-Grade in school. Thankfully my parents loved me enough to *not* give me everything I wanted. And so love (or a kind of love), without truth, is something that injures rather than helps. It is the kind of *love* behind every spoiled-rotten child.

Truth without Love, on the other hand, is like applying the surgeon's scalpel without cleaning, binding, and tending to the wound it leaves. That is why in Ephesians 4:15 it refers to, "speaking the truth in love." There is a desire in some people to 'just tell it like it is.' This kind of statement is often treated like a free-pass to say whatever the speaker wants regardless of the circumstances or people to which they are speaking. While a desire for the truth is right, it must be governed, like all things, by love.

This doesn't mean you don't speak the truth at all times. It simply means you consider how you're speaking it. God is a God of truth and He never lies. Sometimes when He speaks it is of punishment and judgment. His Word divides. Heb 4:12 says, "For the word of God is living and powerful, and sharper than any two-edged sword, piercing even to the division of soul and spirit, and of joints and marrow, and is a discerner of the thoughts and intents of the heart." Truth spoken can and will cause pain at times. But is it the pain that leads to healing?

1 John 4:16 tells us, "And we have known and believed the love that God has for us. **God is love** [emphasis mine], and he who abides in love abides in God, and God in him." When considering the connection between Truth and Love we must understand that God *is* Love. While God *gives* love and does *acts* of love there is a significant difference between human acts of love and God's. God, in His very being is love. Thus, everything that God speaks or does is an expression of His love. In God, Love and Truth are inseparable. And this is why modern tolerance is just a cheap imitation of real love.

Look at marriage for example. Imagine your spouse simply *tolerated* you. This would really be the worst possible state of affairs. It would keep you in perpetual limbo between peace and conflict. It is by no means pleasant to be at odds with your spouse. It can be frustrating, tedious, and even hurtful but it is better than the alternative. A relationship between real people will involve conflict, but conflict leads to resolution. Conflict among people who will speak the truth to themselves and others exposes the rottenness of the heart and leads to life. Tolerance only leads to the living death of an apathetic existence where truth is concealed.

And so, as we are faced with the challenge that Christ brings us we have a choice to make. We can reject Christianity because it is intolerant and exclusive or we can accept it because it is true. We must ask ourselves the honest question. What does exclusivity have to do with whether something is true or false? In reality, truth is always exclusive and narrow. That is truth's essential nature. There are an infinite number of wrong answers to every math problem but only one right. Truth calls to you but you must step out of the shadows and into the light. Cross the line. Embrace truth and find yourself embraced by love.

12

The End of the Road

Throughout this book many thoughts have been offered concerning life, faith, and our responsibility before heaven. It is my sincere hope that something you've read within these pages has kindled an awakening in your spirit towards the God at the beginning of the old road. At the end of this endeavor I am faced with a dilemma as the importance of what I have not said seemingly calls out louder to me than what I have. Alas, the purpose of my writing was not to write a book of Christian theology or even a book of Christian evangelism for that matter.

My desire was to write an appeal to the heart and mind of you the reader to embark upon a journey of rediscovery with regards to the Christian faith. I didn't write this book as a polemic against all I perceive to be wrong with other Christians or even the secular world. I wrote it because I believe the Christian story about the universe and our part to play in it is true. I wrote it because I believe there is a God who desperately loves us and is constantly reaching out towards us. And I believe that He can reach out through the words of a little book. It is often in the unexpected places that God reaches for us.

The mighty biblical prophet Elijah didn't find God in the fire or in the wind but rather in the gentle whisper. Perhaps the faintest whispers have reached your ears? Don't allow the noise of modern life to drown them out. Who can tell if God is speaking gently to your soul? Would you listen if He did?

You might wonder why God, if He really existed, wouldn't just appear and proclaim Himself to you. The statement: "God knows my address," is often heard and it is both true and irrelevant to the question at hand. The real question isn't whether God knows you but rather if you know Him. If the God of the bible really exists than He knows every hair on your head. He has counted every one of your tears and has loved you every day of your life. But He won't just appear.

The End of the Road

His appearing would be like the arrival of the sun in your bedroom; not the light of sun, but the sun itself. The same light that provided you with indisputable proof would also destroy you. It would destroy your capacity to choose, and even worse, your capacity to love. So, our God whispers. You can hear it if you listen.

Appendix: *Thoughts on Heaven*

If a discussion of heaven seems a strange ending to this book I apologize; but it seems to me that heaven is one of the very most important and yet most commonly misunderstood parts of the Christian story. So, the purpose of this brief appendix is twofold. My first aim is to cast down two silly yet common misconceptions of what we call Heaven. The second purpose is to establish in their place an idea of what heaven *may* be like. To be clear, I do not profess to have any concrete knowledge of heaven. I have never been there. My thoughts on heaven will instead be derived from the Holy Scriptures and my own limited understanding of God's nature and His ultimate purpose for mankind.

For many people the thought of heaven brings to mind images of people reclining upon fluffy white clouds gently strumming three-stringed harps while fat little cherubs flutter around them. Several problems immediately present themselves with this conception. First, it seems like a complete waste of time. Second, it seems unbearably boring. Now, these objections may not seem terribly weighty at present but permit me to elaborate.

My problem with this image of heaven and others like it is that they depict an eternity that is without purpose. This I know; heaven will not be a place devoid of purpose. Unless the God of the bible suddenly reversed His nature this kind of heaven would be an impossibility. As the author of Hebrews tells us: "He cannot deny Himself." Remember the God who rushed into history at the beginning of Genesis proclaiming, "Let there be light?" Remember the God of Abraham, Isaac, and Jacob who did miracles among His people? Remember the cross of Christ where He redeemed a people for Himself from sin and death? How could this ever purposeful God who worked tirelessly throughout history abandon purposefulness in the closing act?

We must put this image of a purposeless heaven behind us. To be clear, I am not really dealing with clouds, harps, or cherubs (fat or otherwise). I am dealing with the underlying idea that heaven will consist of eternal leisure and nothing else. From the

Thoughts on Heaven

Scriptures we know heaven will be a place without sorrow or tears but we are never told it will be a place without purposeful occupation. A heaven where we sat on clouds and eternally strummed harps would defy the Scriptures because it would bore us to tears. Now, if we are speaking of using harps to worship the everlasting Lord we have a different story; but I digress.

The problem with a heaven of eternal leisure is that it would quickly cease to be pleasant and morph into a torturous inanity. Many of the world's worst forms of torture involve subjecting the victim to things in extreme measures that they may actually enjoy in the context of freedom. You may enjoy hamburgers but would you enjoy one at every meal for the rest of your life? Perhaps you love the great outdoors but would you trade your bedroom for a cave? What becomes clear is that our pleasures are matters of contrast. I enjoy my sweets because I've eaten my broccoli. A weeklong holiday at the sea is a delight because I've worked all year long in the city. Pleasure without purpose loses its ability to please.

In heaven the streets may be paved with gold but I greatly hope that other features will be made of wood and stone. If everything were made of gold it might as well be made of mud. King Midas would have given all the gold in his kingdom for a cup of cold water. The enjoyment, nay the very existence, of luxury is dependent upon it's sometime being absent. So when we speak of heaven we must use some sense. It won't just be an eternal exercise in frivolity.

A certain atheist is fond of mocking the Christian belief in heaven by calling it "the great theme park in the sky" and then pointing out the silliness of belief in said place. The problem with his challenge isn't that belief in this perpetual pleasure park is justified but rather the fact that this isn't what the Christian faith really teaches about heaven. He has set up a fine straw man to tear down. The problem is that we feed into this negative perception when we speak carelessly about heaven as if it were a purposeless place, or even worse—a place for purposeless people.

We should think about heaven realistically for it is not an unrealistic place. There is no such thing as an unrealistic place which actually exists. Sometimes truth is stranger than fiction. If heaven is a *real* place than it is totally realistic but this in no way means that it isn't fantastic. Many real places and things are fantastic. The ocean is a fantastic place but it is also real. The planet Jupiter is fantastic and every bit as real as the corner store. So it is with heaven. It is a *really* fantastic place. We should not shy away from thinking or speaking about the potential wonders of heaven but we should do this with the seriousness that betokens our eventual arrival. What will I see when I get to heaven? Or, more importantly, what will I be when I get to heaven?

The second misconception I wish to deal with is the idea that heaven will be a place where we are all thrown together into some kind of a cosmic oneness with God, each other, the universe, etc. where we lose our identity. I protest that this idea has snuck in from the eastern religions and perhaps Greek philosophy and has no place in the Christian faith. One of the really holy and fearful things about the Christian faith is the value and responsibility it places on the individual. By individuals I mean you, me, and everyone else. Christianity tells us that we were created in the likeness and image of God. Every one of us is fearfully and wonderfully made. I think when we really grasp this truth our understanding of heaven will be deepened. God doesn't want to throw us away. We are not garbage to be recycled but rather treasures being restored.

Heaven isn't a place where we become less than who we are now but rather more. C.S. Lewis famously described this temporal earthly existence as the shadow lands, inferring that heaven is the truly real place; the place where we will come into ourselves rather than lose ourselves. God didn't make any two people exactly alike. Every person that has ever lived, is living, and will live in the future has a unique soul. And every person has an eternal soul. We won't cease to be who we are in heaven. We will be the perfected versions of ourselves, or I should say, the originally intended versions.

Now having dealt with these two misconceptions we can begin to explore what heaven may be like. In dealing with these two fallacies we have uncovered two truths. Number one, heaven is a purposeful place. Number two, people have tremendous and unique value which will be preserved and enhanced. Taking these things together I think it safe to say that we won't have less of a life in heaven then we have now. If the depth of our lives on earth, in the shadow lands if you will, is any indicator of how complex heaven will be than we are in for something exciting.

We should stop thinking of this life as the reality and heaven as the dream because it's really the other way round. What will it be like to have a perfect resurrected body and a spotless soul? What will it be like to fellowship with God with no barrier between us? We cannot imagine the pleasure and the thrill of becoming our true selves. And what does it mean to become our true selves? It means we will be restored to our original purpose and place within God's creation. In the new heaven and earth we will be as we were intended to be. One thing is sure. We will be restored to perfect relationship with God and will enjoy His presence. We will worship. We will know Him and be known by Him.

We will also know and be known by other people in heaven. All relationships will be free of the maladies that plague us here on earth such as fear, jealously, insecurity, and misunderstanding. Imagine the joy of perfect fellowship with others as well as God. We shouldn't fear the loss of our earthly relationships but instead anticipate their perfection and fulfillment. There will not be less love in heaven but rather more.

As I end this brief treatise on heaven I must ask for your forgiveness for I have perhaps kindled a curiosity within you which no earthly thing can satisfy: a longing to know more about heaven. I do not apologize for kindling a desire for that place; we should all seek that, but rather for the intellectual curiosity of what heaven will be like. For analogy we can ponder the nearly unquenchable curiosity of a child in the waning weeks of December as Christmas approaches. The neatly wrapped parcels under the tree tantalize the imagination with vivid visions of the presents within. It is the elongated, almost tortuous period of anticipation which produces the rapturous delight on Christmas morning when the presents are opened.

I believe that our amazingly good Father has really outdone Himself when it comes to heaven. Apart from all analogies we really are in the waning years of this earthly existence whether we are young or old. Eternity approaches at the speed of time and for those of us who are the children of this great Father the wait can be agonizing. The scriptures tantalize our imaginations with descriptions of a place without pain or sorrow, streets of gold, and the people we've loved and lost to death waiting for us. This place, this fantastic place, beckons us vaguely yet powerfully; quickening a passion that has no earthly resolution.

As we cast our eyes upon the present reality we see the unfulfilled dreams, broken promises, and often painful circumstances we live in. Juxtaposed against this dim backdrop is heaven in all of its radiant majesty, wreathed in clouds of glory that obscure it from our sight. Whatever heaven is, it will surely be a surprise and therein lays a great deal of the joy. The thrill of the unknown hangs like a curtain to be pulled back when we cross from death to life or Christ returns to pull it back along with the eastern sky.

The End

Continue the journey @

www.jacobschmelzer.com

www.zoebiblecollege.com

37106940R00083

Made in the USA
Charleston, SC
27 December 2014